Below: sunset over Swaledale, close to the village of Keld.

Right: a field barn near Bainbridge.

- THE -
YORKSHIRE DALES

John Potter

MYRIAD

Left: the tiny hamlet of Keld nestles snugly in the hills at the head of Swaledale and stands at the crossroads of the coast-to-coast and Pennine Way long-distance footpaths. Ten minutes' stroll north of the village, there is a series of four waterfalls – Kisdon Force, East Gill Force (shown here), Catrake Force and Wain Wath Force, all fed by the many becks which run into the river Swale.

Right: the largest settlement in Arkengarthdale, Langthwaite's stone cottages huddle together haphazardly alongside Arkle Beck, three miles north-west of Reeth. The welcoming Red Lion pub in the village was used extensively in the filming of the television series *All Creatures Great and Small*. There is a steep single track lane up towards Booze (ironically, a village without a pub!) where walkers can soak up the panoramic views across Arkengarthdale.

The limestone mass of Kisdon Hill stands at the western head of Swaledale. This viewpoint is from Kisdon Hill looking south towards Muker with the river Swale meandering through the valley to the left.

Left: the pretty village of Muker sits proudly above Straw Beck just before it joins the river Swale one mile east of Thwaite. The church of St Mary the Virgin is at the heart of the village. Its beautiful stained glass depicts the surrounding scenery and includes an image of 23 horned sheep – a reference to Psalm 23, *The Lord is my Shepherd*.

Right: situated 12 miles west of Richmond, Reeth was once a centre for both leadmining and knitting; it is still a market town and focal point for the local community. From its elevated position the spacious, triangular village green provides stunning views of the surrounding countryside. The Swaledale Museum on the green houses exhibits showing the heritage of the area; it is open during the summer months. The Reeth agricultural show is held in August.

Left: the busy market town of Hawes is situated between high fells at the head of Wensleydale, on the trans-Pennine A684 that links Northallerton in North Yorkshire to Kendal in Cumbria. Known as the "little capital" of Upper Wensleydale, it is Yorkshire's highest market town. This beautiful field barn lies close to the town.

Right: the capital of Swaledale, Richmond is dominated by its majestic castle keep, a well-preserved example of 12th-century architecture. The town lies south-west of Scotch Corner on the A6108 and is one of the most beautiful in England, with elegant Georgian houses, cobbled streets and pretty cottage gardens. At the centre of the marketplace is the 12th-century chapel of the Holy Trinity, now the regimental museum of the Green Howards.

Situated half a mile north of Hawes, Gayle is a quiet and pretty village. At the foot of Sledale, Duerley Beck cascades over a series of limestone steps in the centre of the village before rushing below a packhorse bridge.

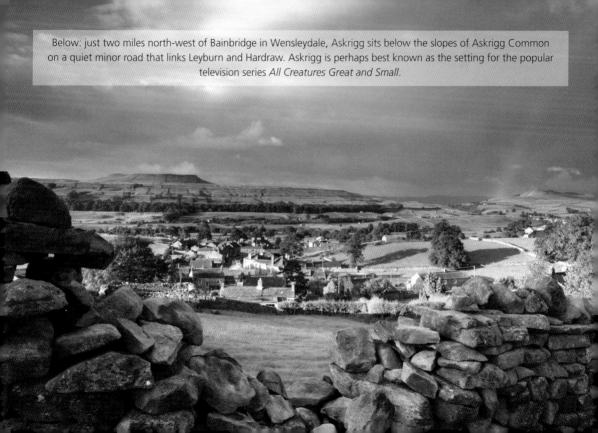

Below: just two miles north-west of Bainbridge in Wensleydale, Askrigg sits below the slopes of Askrigg Common on a quiet minor road that links Leyburn and Hardraw. Askrigg is perhaps best known as the setting for the popular television series *All Creatures Great and Small*.

Left: the village of Aysgarth is situated seven miles west of Leyburn and is best known for its spectacular waterfalls that cascade down a series of large limestone steps, making it one of Wensleydale's most popular attractions. A series of delightful riverside walks link the Upper, Middle and Lower Aysgarth Falls. Known collectively as Aysgarth Force, the three sets of falls are all within one mile of each other. The best view of the Upper Force is from the 16th-century bridge which spans the river Ure.

Right: the pretty, unspoiled village of West Burton is situated one mile south of Aysgarth on the B6160 at the northern end of Bishopdale. To the east of the village the glorious West Burton Falls, known locally as Cauldron Falls, are best seen from the footbridge at the north end of West Burton. After heavy rainfall, the picturesque falls become a raging torrent as Walden Beck fills with rainwater. The annual May Fair, on the village green, is a popular event for both locals and visitors.

Above: just two miles south of Leyburn, Middleham is dominated by its castle, which can be seen for miles around. It was built around 1170 by Robert Fitz Randolph during the reign of Henry II. The keep has 12ft (3.5m) thick walls.

Right: Bolton Castle is best known for the fortress of Castle Bolton which stands on the western edge of the village. This massive structure was built in 1379. The attractive 14th-century church of St Oswald's nestles in its shadow.

The Howgills are a small distinctive group of rounded hills bordered by Sedbergh, Kirkby Stephen and Tebay. The southern half of the Howgills lie in the Yorkshire Dales National Park, whilst the northern Howgills are in Cumbria.

Above: with its white-painted houses and softly rounded fells, Dentdale has many of the typical characteristics of the Lake District. The pretty village of Dent boasts the highest mainline railway station in Britain (four miles from the village) and is close to the spectacular viaducts of Arten Gill and Dent Head.

Right: the church of St Mary in Ingleton. This pretty market town nestles in the lee of Ingleborough, one of the famous Three Peaks. The Ingleton waterfalls provide visitors with the spectacular sight of a series of cascades tumbling down through wooded gorges.

Above: these two boulders are in the heart of Three Peaks limestone country. Called the Cheese Press Stones, they remind us of the time when cheese was pressed into shape between large stones to dry out.

Right: the 72-mile Settle to Carlisle railway line is widely considered the most scenic rail route in Britain. The magnificent Ribblehead Viaduct was built between 1870-1875 and is 1200ft long.

Right: Settle is a busy market town with a quite dramatic setting. It sits snugly between the river Ribble and Castlebergh, an impressive 300ft (91m) limestone crag; its pretty market square is surrounded by 18th and 19th-century houses, shops and eateries – including the Naked Man Café (right). The Settle to Carlisle railway line starts from nearby Settle Junction; from the magnificent Ribblehead Viaduct there are dramatic views of Whernside and Pen-y-Ghent.

Left: the little village of Clapham, just off the busy A65 six miles north-west of Settle, is a blissful haven for visitors. It is the perfect base for exploring remote and beautiful Crummackdale and is a focal point for walks to Selside, Austwick and Horton in Ribblesdale.

Right above: a Dales' scene taken in midwinter, close to Horton in Ribblesdale.

Right: taken from the Pennine Way long-distance footpath on the remote Stainforth to Littondale road, this dramatic view of Pen-y-Ghent almost entices the walker to tackle this famous peak.

Malhamdale is popular with visitors. It contains some of Britain's most beautiful and spectacular limestone features such as Malham Cove, Gordale Scar, Janet's Foss Waterfall and Malham Tarn. Malham Cove is just three-quarters of a mile north of the village of Malham, and at 250ft (76m) high and over 300 yards (275m) long, is a magnificent vertical limestone rockface.

Above: Arncliffe lies at the heart of Littondale and is the largest of the four settlements in the dale, which include the village of Litton and the hamlets of Halton Gill and Foxup. The village has a central green, surrounded by stone cottages and farm buildings.

Just one mile north-east of Malham, the limestone escarpment opens up into a huge rocky gorge known as Gordale Scar. This massive ravine is one of the most spectacular sights in the Dales.

Littondale and Wharfedale from Hill Castle Scar. This photograph was taken just a few metres from the Dales Way long-distance footpath, between Kettlewell and Grassington, just north-east of the delightful village of Conistone in Wharfedale.

Left: Yockenthwaite is a tiny settlement in Langstrothdale nestling on the hillside beside the infant river Wharfe. In Norman times Langstrothdale Chase was a hunting preserve for game and deer; now the upper dale is a haven of solitude with a scattering of stone barns and traditional Dales' cottages.

Right and below: Hubberholme is located on the Dales Way at the foot of Langstrothdale. It is famous for the atmospheric George Inn and the beautiful church of St Michael's. The choir stalls and the pews were made in 1934 by Robert Thompson, the "Mouseman" of Kilburn.

Left: the little hamlet of Cray nestles at the southern end of Bishopdale one and a half miles north of Buckden. It is the starting point for many walks and its famous inn, The White Lion, is the highest pub in Wharfedale. Cray Gill runs into the river Wharfe a couple of miles south of the village and is fed by several smaller gills.

Below: four miles north of Kettlewell, Buckden is the perfect base for exploring Wharfedale. Thousands of visitors visit the area to see the spectacular wildflower meadows which surround the village in spring.

Great Whernside dominates the skyline to the east of Buckden. The long boulder-strewn ridge gives extensive views across Nidderdale to the east and westward to Wharfedale.

Left and above: in the shadow of Great Whernside, clustered close to Cam Beck, near where it joins the river Wharfe, Kettlewell is popular with potholers, climbers and walkers. The fields above lie just south of the village.

Right: the characterful stone cottages of Linton cluster around a large village green, with the welcoming Fontaine Inn at its centre. Pretty riverside paths carry walkers along both banks of Linton Beck with its attractive stepping stone bridge.

One of the most photographed of all the Dales' villages, Burnsall, 10 miles north-west of Ilkley, is famous for its massive five-arched bridge, which spans the river Wharfe.

Right and below: the largest settlement in upper Wharfedale, the village of Grassington owes its development to its close proximity to the point where two historically important roads cross in the dale – the B6160 from Ilkley to Buckden and the B6265 Skipton to Pateley Bridge. Grassington has many charming features including a cobbled square complete with an ornate water pump. The village grew rapidly with the opening of the Yorkshire Dales Railway to Threshfield in 1901; it transported the settlers who worked in nearby Skipton or in one of the limestone quarries which developed in the area.

Left: located in an upland valley two miles east of Grassington, the small village of Hebden sits in a narrow gorge above Hebden Beck. A quaint packhorse bridge leads over the beck to a cluster of tiny cottages on the far bank.

Right and below: Bolton Bridge, five miles west of Skipton, is the gateway to Wharfedale. Close by is the beautiful Augustinian priory of Bolton Abbey. It is a popular picnic spot and visitors often spend the whole day by the river.

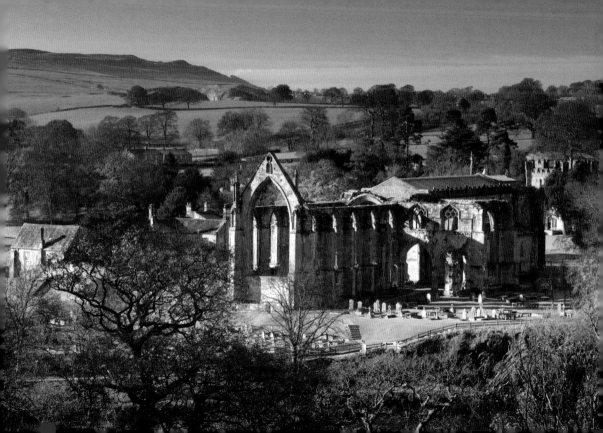

Left: Pateley Bridge in upper Nidderdale is surrounded by beautiful countryside. The town's narrow main street is dominated by elegant dark gritstone buildings with pretty cobbled alleyways and passages which lead to hidden and quaint courtyards.

Right and below: Skipton Castle is one of the best-preserved medieval castles in England. The Leeds-Liverpool Canal lies a few minutes walk from the high street. The canal helped establish the worsted cloth industry in the town.

Right: the village of West Tanfield sits beside the river Ure on the western edge of the Yorkshire Dales, just six miles north of Ripon. The skyline of the village is dominated by the Marmion Tower and the church of St Nicholas.

Below: the cobbled marketplace at Masham is surrounded by elegant Georgian houses and stone cottages. The town is famous for the annual Masham Steam Engine Rally.

Right: one of Yorkshire's most popular attractions, Fountains Abbey and Studley Royal is a huge estate which includes the largest ruined abbey in England, together with a spectacular Georgian water garden and deer park.

Below: the beautiful ruins of Jervaulx Abbey lie between Masham and Leyburn. The abbey was founded in 1156 by Cistercian monks who moved from Fors, higher up the valley.

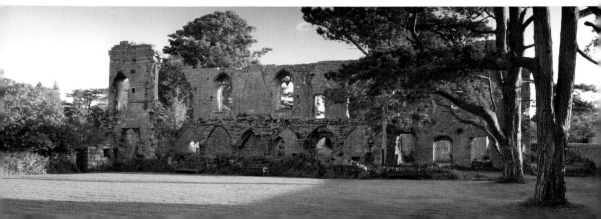

Below and right: the small city of Ripon lies on the banks of the river Ure and is regarded as a gateway to the eastern Dales. Behind its attractive riverside houses is Ripon Cathedral. St Wilfred first built a church here over 1,300 years ago but the present building is the fourth to be established on this site. The church did not achieve cathedral status until 1836 when the diocese of Ripon was created. The western front and towers of the cathedral are fine examples of early English church architecture. The Decorated nave was built in the 15th century. Ripon has three museums – the Courthouse Museum, the Prison and Police Museum and the Workhouse Museum of Poor Law.

The tiny hamlet of Foxup in Littondale is made up of a scattering of small cottages and farms close to where Foxup Beck feeds the infant river Skirfare.